W9-ADX-999

EDUCATION
LIBRARY

QUEEN'S UNIVERSITY
AT KINGSTON

KINGSTON ONTARIO CANADA

20.95

Junk in Space

Richard Maurer

Simon and Schuster Books for Young Readers
Published by Simon & Schuster Inc., New York

In association with WGBH Boston,
producers of NOVA for public television

SIMON AND SCHUSTER
BOOKS FOR YOUNG READERS
Simon & Schuster Building
Rockefeller Center
1230 Avenue of the Americas
New York, NY 10020

Copyright © 1989 by Richard Maurer
and WGBH Educational Foundation

All rights reserved including the right of
reproduction in whole or in part in any form.
SIMON AND SCHUSTER
BOOKS FOR YOUNG READERS
is a trademark of Simon & Schuster Inc.

Manufactured in Spain.

10 9 8 7 6 5 4 3 2 1
10 9 8 7 6 5 4 3 2 1 (pbk.)

Library of Congress
Cataloging-in-Publication Data
Maurer, Richard, 1950.
Junk in space/Richard Maurer.
(A NOVABOOK)
"In association with WGBH Boston,
producers of NOVA for public television."
Includes index.
Summary: Describes space trash; from
mislaid cameras and tools to abandoned
satellites and moon vehicles, and includes
sections on how they got there, potential
hazards to navigation, orbits, etc.
1. Space debris–Juvenile literature.
[1. Space debris.].
I. WGBH (Television station :
Boston, Mass.)
II. NOVA (Television program)
III. Title. IV. Series.
TL 1489.M38 1989
363.7'28'0919 – dc1989-30060 CIP AC

ISBN 0-671-67768-3
ISBN 0-671-67767-5 (pbk.)

Illustration from *The Little Prince* by
Antoine de Saint-Exupéry, copyright 1943
and renewed 1971 by Harcourt Brace
Jovanovich, Inc., reprinted by permission of
the publisher.

This book is for Joe.

Mission control on this project
was WGBH Boston, where
Karen Johnson, Nancy Lat-
tanzio, Marianne Neuman, and
Cheryl LeBlanc-Dooley handled
the editorial and administrative
duties, and Douglass Scott,
Christopher Pullman, and M J
Walsh handled the design and
typesetting. I am grateful to each
of them – and also to Matthew
Bartholomew, who produced
the illustrations, and Paula
Apsell, executive producer of
NOVA.

I extend my thanks as well
to Simon Boughton and his
co-workers at the Simon &
Schuster Children's Book Division, and to the many NASA,
Air Force, and other space spe-
cialists who answered my ques-
tions. Among the last group, I
am especially grateful to J. Kelly
Beatty and Nicholas L. Johnson
who reviewed the manuscript.

Finally, I thank Susie, Sam,
and Joe, who contributed their
enthusiasm, encouragement,
and endearing distraction.

The NOVA television series is
produced by WGBH Boston.
Funding for the series is
provided by public television
stations, the Johnson & Johnson
Family of Companies, and
Lockheed Corporation.

Title page:
**An "angry alligator" greets
astronauts during a space
rendezvous in 1966. Nose
cones are usually discarded
before rockets reach orbit, but
this one didn't come off.**

▶
**Junk-collecting in space,
1984. Two astronauts from
the U.S. space shuttle re-
trieve a communications
satellite stranded in a useless orbit.**

Contents

Into the Unknown

Over a hundred years ago, the French writer Jules Verne produced a remarkable tale about a ship that could dive to the ocean bottom. The story, *Twenty Thousand Leagues Under the Sea,* told of the mysterious Captain Nemo who cruised beneath the world in his submarine *Nautilus.*

Since this was long before practical submarines and diving equipment had been invented, Verne's readers were eager to learn what lay in the ocean depths, where no one had ever been. And what Verne described was eerie. The seafloor, as he told it, was littered everywhere with the debris of civilization. Everything ever sunk in the oceans was preserved down below as if in a museum.

The author was mainly interested in describing the famous shipwrecks. Here was a fleet of treasure ships lost off the Spanish coast in 1702. Further out to sea, the *Nautilus* found the *Revenge,* a French warship sunk by the British in 1794. Well-traveled routes like the English Channel, the Mediterranean, and the Gulf of Saint Lawrence were littered with sunken vessels. But almost everywhere the *Nautilus* found odd bits of chain, cannon shot, and ships' instruments.

The *Nautilus* surveys junk on the sea bottom in a nineteenth-century engraving from *Twenty Thousand Leagues Under the Sea.* The "league" of the title is a unit of distance equal to 3½ miles (5.6 km). The 20,000 leagues were traveled around the earth – not straight down.

◄ The *Solar Max* scientific satellite in orbit 310 miles (500 km) above the earth, after being repaired by a crew from the U.S. space shuttle in 1984.

No doubt, Jules Verne exaggerated how often you are likely to stumble on a shipwreck in the wide ocean. But the voyage of the *Nautilus* serves as a reminder that nothing is truly lost in the vastness of the sea.

In our own day, this is equally true of another ocean. Since 1957, almost 4,000 satellite payloads have been launched into space. Many of these, orbiting near the earth, have fallen into the atmosphere and disintegrated – like ships driven against the rocks. But others are safely in deep space, destined to orbit for thousands if not millions of years.

A *Nautilus* of the future will find no shortage of shipwrecks in space: here, an old weather station; there, a navigation beacon; on the moon, campsites of the original explorers; odd bolts, cylinders, and other junk everywhere; and at the farthest ends of the solar system, a few vessels drifting outward to the stars.

In this book, we will voyage, like the *Nautilus*, into the dark unknown sea that surrounds our planet, to explore the museum of relics in space.

Space Glossary

Satellite: One object that orbits another. The space shuttle, when in space, is a satellite of the earth. The earth, in turn, is a satellite of the sun.

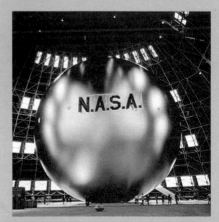

An unusual payload: *Echo 1,* a giant balloon inflated in orbit and then used to reflect radio signals. It is seen here during an inflation test on the ground in 1960.

Rocket: A device that shoots gasses in one direction in order to travel in the other. Rockets are ideal for reaching orbital speeds. Once there, they are switched off.

Payload: The cargo carried by a rocket. If your intention is to put an orange into space, that is your payload.

Spacecraft: A payload designed to operate independently in space. A spacecraft can usually send and receive radio signals, generate its own power, and change its position with small thrusters.

Space junk: Broken, discarded, or useless objects in space. If it would be considered junk on the ground, it's definitely junk in space.

A typical spacecraft: *Landsat 4,* an earth resources satellite being checked out before launch in 1982.

7,122 and Counting

On September 29, 1988, the U.S. space shuttle returned to orbit after the long delay caused by the *Challenger* accident in 1986. But what else went up during that September? And what came down?

The month got off to a bad start when a secret U.S. Air Force satellite was boosted into a useless orbit on September 2. But three days later the military bounced back by successfully launching a four-part payload for tracking ships. China had a success the following day with a weather satellite, as did the Soviet Union with a spy satellite. On September 8, the European Space Agency put two American communications satellites aloft. Disaster struck, though, when one of the payloads misfired and went into the wrong orbit.

The next week belonged to the Soviets who sent up an earth resources satellite, a supply ship for their human-occupied space station, another spy satellite, and three navigation orbiters. The Japanese joined in on the 16th with a communications satellite. And on the 19th, a new country entered space when Israel launched its first payload, an engineering test satellite.

Yet another Soviet spy satellite followed on the 22nd. A U.S. weather satellite was launched on the 24th. And finally, on September 29, hours before the shuttle took off with its communications payload to deposit in orbit, the Soviets sent up one of their own communications craft. So ended a month in the space business.

Less glamorous were the objects that accompanied these orbiters into space: a total of forty-five rocket parts, plus hundreds of insulation strips, metal fragments, and other trash too tiny to detect with radar.

What goes up must come down, and an average of twenty objects a week reentered during September. Two cosmonauts returned in a ferry ship from the Soviet space station (making news when they were almost stranded in orbit). Four camera capsules from Soviet spy and earth-resources craft parachuted into central Asia. And eighty-one odds and ends of orbiting junk reentered the atmosphere in a blaze of fire (not having protective heat shields, it all burned up on the way down).

Still orbiting the earth were a total of 1,734 payloads, some dating to the beginning of the space age. Only about 350 were working. Another 5,388 pieces of orbiting debris were being tracked.

The space census as of midnight September 30, 1988: 7,122 objects – one of which was the U.S. space shuttle, still on its shakedown cruise and not due to return until October 3. Also up there: a few hundred other objects which showed up on radar but which busy space watchers had not had time to catalog.

The U.S. space shuttle blasts off during a busy month for spaceflight: September 1988.

Space Lanes

▶
A three-stage rocket climbs part way up earth's gravity sink. The first stage makes a perfect parabola – like a McDonald's arch. At the top of the arch, the second stage takes over. By the time the third stage has fired (making the short, bright trail at the very top), the vehicle is at an altitude of 550 miles (880 km). Although this is well within the zone of orbiting satellites, the rocket is not designed to reach orbital speed and so falls back to earth. The two bright clouds show where the rocket released chemicals to map the magnetic field that causes the northern lights; the "lights" are visible as a whispy glow spanning the sky. The many short tracks show the paths of the stars in this seven-minute exposure.

The sea of space begins a hundred miles (160 km) or so above our planet. Here, far above the mountaintops and clouds, higher than the highest-flying jet planes, the atmosphere thins to almost nothing, and the realm of orbiting space vehicles takes over.

Orbits are the sea lanes of space. Back in the days of sailing ships, sailors followed winds along routes that were seldom straight-line courses to their destinations. In a similar way, objects in space follow curved routes called orbits. Orbits are the only way to travel anywhere in space, and it will be worth our effort to understand them.

Gravity Sinks

Imagine a deep, round sink with a ball at the bottom. A small sideways push sends the ball arching up the side of the basin and then back down. If the ball is pushed with more force, it will spin around and around the inside, like a bicycle racing around a banked track, until friction (the rubbing of one thing against another) slows it and it rolls to the bottom. An even faster push will send it spinning higher up the side. Faster still and it will be propelled out of the sink altogether. (You can try this yourself. If you don't have a round sink, a large mixing bowl works well.)

Each of these cases corresponds to a rocket leaving the gravity "sink" of the earth at different speeds.

In the first case, the rocket simply shoots up into the sky and falls back. This is the trajectory of a Fourth-of-July rocket, for example.

In the second case, the rocket has enough speed to balance exactly the force pulling it back, and it goes into orbit around the earth. With more speed, it goes into a higher orbit. This corresponds to a satellite launch. The faster the launch velocity, the higher the orbit.

In the last case, the rocket escapes from the earth's gravity altogether. But into what? Into a much larger sink, as it turns out. The earth is itself in orbit part way up the side of this huge gravity sink, and spaced up and down the side are the other eight planets of the solar system. This bigger basin is, of course, the gravity field of the sun. Launching into this realm starts our rocket on an interplanetary voyage.

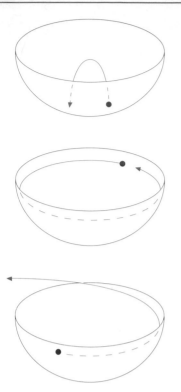

▲
**The path of a rocket under the influ-
ence of gravity can be simulated with
a ball in a sink. A small push (top)
sends the ball up and then back. A
stronger push (middle) propels the
ball around and around, as if in orbit.
Stronger still (bottom), and the ball
escapes – like a rocket leaving
earth's gravitational field.**

▶
**A model of the sun's gravitational
field. The force of gravity causes objects to behave as if they are traveling
inside a huge sink. A critical speed –
the "orbital" speed – is needed to
keep from falling to the bottom of the
sink. The planets have their own
gravitational fields, which are inset in
the sun's much larger one.**

If our rocket's speed has been precisely the amount needed to get it over the rim of the earth's gravity sink, and no more, the spaceship will simply travel together with the earth in the same orbit around the sun. To reach a planet "higher up" in the sun's gravity sink – Mars, Jupiter, Saturn, Uranus, Neptune, or Pluto – the rocket must speed up into a higher solar orbit. To reach a planet "lower down" – Venus or Mercury – the rocket must put on the brakes and fall into a lower solar orbit. "Putting on the brakes" means firing a rocket against the direction of travel in order to lose orbital speed.

Though we have been speaking here of rockets traveling in orbits, the rocket itself (that is, the propulsion system) is needed only to get into orbit or, once there, to change orbits. Once the vehicle is in its final orbit, the rocket motor is no longer needed. On the earth's surface a vehicle must continually fight air and road resistance to stay moving. But in space there are almost no sources of friction to slow a vehicle down. Satellites that orbit near the top of the earth's atmosphere – up to an altitude of about 300 miles (500 km) – do need an occasional boost to fight the friction caused by collisions with stray air molecules. But aside from that and a few other small frictional effects, space vehicles are on an effortless ride.

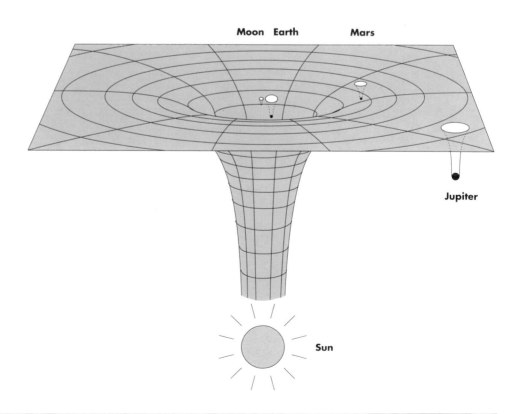

Ellipses

One feature of orbits is that they are almost always ellipses of some sort, varying from circles to ovals. An ellipse is a geometric figure that can be created by tacking the two ends of a piece of string so that the string is slack, then pulling a pencil taut against the string and drawing a line all the way around the fixed points. The result is an elongated circle; the more separated the two points are, the more elongated (or elliptical) the final figure will be. If the points are directly on top of each other, the resulting shape will be a circle.

A circle is the simplest kind of ellipse. It is also the simplest kind of orbit. A spacecraft revolving at a constant distance up the wall of a gravity sink traces out a circle. Because the spacecraft never varies its distance from the object it is orbiting and is therefore under a constant gravitational pull, its speed is also constant.

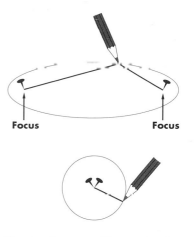

Focus   Focus

How to draw an ellipse: attach a piece of string at two "focus" points and slide the pencil along the string. If the points are at the same spot, you will get a circle.

Down the Sink

"What goes up must come down."

So goes the common sense notion of gravity. But of course it's more complicated than that. If we lived on a planet as small as the Little Prince's planet in the story by Saint Exupéry (it was an asteroid no larger than a house), almost nothing would come down once it was set moving. In fact, the planet itself would probably be pulled toward a larger planet nearby – crashing into it!

What we call gravity is the attraction of everything for everything else. Two people six feet (2 m) apart gravitate toward each other, so to speak, but the force is so small – less than a millionth of an ounce (or about 0.01 mg) – that it's too weak to overcome the resistance of their feet against the floor. On the other hand, the earth exerts a hefty gravitational force that everyone feels, though we often forget about it. Slip on the ice and you will remember it soon enough.

Gravitational force, then, depends on the size of an object, or more precisely, on its mass, which is the amount of matter it contains. Earth is one hundred billion trillion (100,000,000,000,000,000,000,000) times more massive than the average human. And so the earth exerts that much more force on a person than a person does on the earth.

The gravitational attraction between objects falls off rapidly as the distance between them increases. At twice the distance (measured from the center of a spherical object like the earth) the attraction is one-quarter as strong; at three times the distance, one-ninth as strong; and at ten times the distance, one one-hundreth.

The Little Prince at home on Asteroid B-612. The prince would probably weigh about 35 pounds (16 kg) on earth, but he weighs only one ten-thousandth of an ounce (30 mg) on his home planet – assuming it has the same density as the earth. A sneeze would send him flying into space.

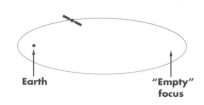

Earth   "Empty" focus

An elliptical orbit. Earth is at one focus. The other focus is empty.

But if a satellite revolves around a gravity sink at an angle, going high up one side of the sink and low down the other, it traces out an ellipse. The more tilted the trajectory, the more elliptical the orbit. One way you can picture this is to take any circular shape, like a coin, hold it facing you, and then close one eye. It looks circular. Now tilt it slightly. It looks elliptical. Tilt it even more and it looks more elliptical.

A satellite in an elliptical orbit is under a continually changing pull of gravity – like a rubber band being flexed. As the spacecraft climbs up the wall of the sink, fighting gravity, it gradually slows until it hasn't enough speed to climb any higher. At this point, it's at the top of the ellipse. Then it begins to fall back, reaching its greatest speed (and its closest point to the object it is orbiting) as it races around the bottom of the ellipse. The spacecraft then has enough energy to shoot back up the wall again.

Mathematics is a tidy subject, and the source of gravity at the very bottom of our sink does not correspond to just any random point on the inside of a particular orbit. It will always be one of the two points (called the focus points) where you would tack the ends of a piece of string to create that particular orbital ellipse. In the case of a circular orbit, the source of gravity is at the center of the circle. The orbits of most of the planets, though slightly elliptical, can hardly be distinguished from circles. The sun, of course, is the source of gravity at the center.

Transfer Orbits

Ellipses and circles are to orbits what winds and currents are to the sea lanes. You have to know how to use them if you want to get anywhere.

For example, say that you wish to get from the earth to Mars. Both are in roughly circular orbits around the sun. But you don't just hop from one to the other in a single bound. Your rocket must first escape from the earth's gravity, adding enough extra velocity to carry you on an elliptical orbit up to Mars. Timing is important because you want Mars to be at the spot where your spacecraft crosses the planet's orbit. At the very top of the ellipse, your vehicle is moving too slowly to stay at Mars's altitude and will begin to fall unless you do something. Simply fire your rocket engines to come up to Mars's speed. You will enter an identical, circular orbit around the sun. Then, if you wish, you can put on the brakes to descend into Mars's own gravity sink.

This two-step procedure – first boost into an elliptical transfer orbit, then adjust to a circular orbit at the desired altitude – is often used by space vehicles that need to reach a circular orbit. The elliptical transfer orbit by itself is useful if you're interested in just flying by a particular planet or some other point without stopping.

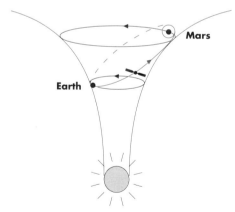

Getting from earth to Mars requires an elliptical transfer orbit that connects the orbits of the two planets. On arrival at Mars, the spacecraft can either: continue past on the dotted trajectory, fire its rocket to enter an identical solar orbit with Mars, expend more energy to enter Mars orbit (as shown), or burn even longer to land on the planet.

Orbits can be quite complicated, but we have covered the basic rules. You can think of spaceflight as taking place inside a huge sink, or along some other curved surface. But the point is that everything in space moves in orbits under the influence of gravity. Gravity, in a sense, "bends" space so that the easiest course is seldom a straight line, but a curved one – an orbit.

Captain Nemo's travels aboard the *Nautilus* took him along the major shipping routes of his day, which explains why he encountered so many shipwrecks. Our voyage in search of spacewrecks will take us across the major orbital routes, coasting along the space lanes.

Rules of the Road

Orbit Rule #1: Orbits are ellipses (which include circles). The object being orbited will be at one of the focus points of the ellipse.

Orbit Rule #2: Orbits can be in any direction. An earth satellite can orbit in the direction that the earth turns, or in the opposite direction. The orbit can be along the equator, over the poles, or at any angle in between.

Orbit Rule #3: The time to complete an orbit around the earth depends on the average altitude of the satellite. The higher the satellite, the longer it takes to complete the orbit.

These rules, in turn, relate to three sets of numbers used to specify a particular orbit. We will call them "settings" (though space engineers refer to them as "elements").

Orbit Setting #1: *Apogee* and *perigee* . These are the farthest and nearest points to earth's surface reached during the orbit. Being directly opposite each other on the orbital ellipse, the apogee and perigee tell how elliptical the orbit is. An orbit with a 25,000-mile (40,000-km) apogee and a 100-mile (160-km) perigee is very elliptical indeed, while an orbit with apogee and perigee at the same height is a perfect circle.

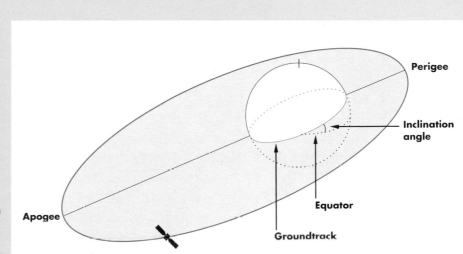

Orbit Setting #2: *Inclination*, or the angle (or tilt) of the orbit. The inclination is measured relative to the equator and determines how much of the globe will pass beneath a satellite. A satellite that crosses the equator at 90 degrees (a right angle) will fly directly over the north and south poles; as the earth spins beneath the orbit, all points on the globe will eventually pass beneath it. By contrast, a satellite that crosses at 0 degrees (no angle) orbits directly over the equator and will never fly over points to the north or south. Notice that the inclination angle is the same as the maximum latitude (or east-west line on the earth's surface) reached by the satellite: 0 degrees latitude is the equator; 90 degrees corresponds to the poles.

The parts of an orbit. The "ground-track" is the path on the earth's surface directly beneath the satellite.

Orbit Setting #3: *Period*, or the time to complete an orbit. Orbital periods for earth satellites vary from eighty-eight minutes for the lowest orbiters to about a month for objects as high as the moon. The period is calculated from the "semi-major axis," which is the total of the apogee height plus the perigee height plus the diameter of the earth, all divided by two.

By following these basic rules and adjusting the different settings of apogee, perigee, inclination, and period, engineers can come up with the perfect orbit to suit their space mission.

The Shallows

The nautical chart at lower left traces a section of the voyage of the *Nautilus* in *Twenty Thousand Leagues Under the Sea*. The dots show a sampling of shipwrecks in the region. Most wrecks hug the coasts – the shallows where 98 percent of all sea disasters occur.

At the lower right is our chart for this chapter. Like the *Nautilus*, we will cross the congested shallows – for us, the near-earth orbital lanes – and head out into the deep, where the dots marking wrecks are few and far between.

In the chapters that follow, our journey will continue past the moon, down toward the sun, and then up the wall of the solar gravity sink to its very rim. The products of our technology have spread very far indeed.

A few of the dots on the chart mark the sites of working spacecraft. But only a few. Of the many thousands of catalogued objects in space, only a few hundred are functioning at any given time. Everything else is junk.

What sort of junk? To find out, let's look at what happens when a rocket leaves the earth for space. Remember that a rocket is simply a transportation system for putting a payload into a particular orbit. After that it is usually thrown away.

(Below left) The locations of some of the many shipwrecks off the coast of North America. If all wrecks were shown, the near-shore waters would be solid with dots. The route of the *Nautilus* is shown in red.

(Below right) The locations of objects in orbit around the earth on October 14, 1988. Fewer than one in ten is a working spacecraft.

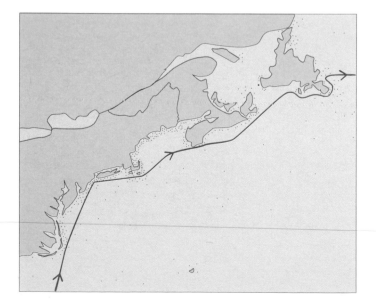

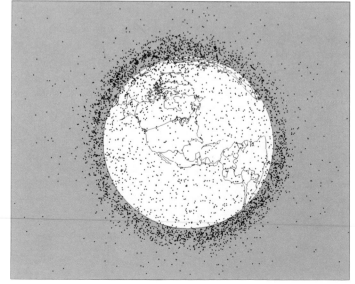

Steps into Space

A typical three-stage rocket takes off with a spacecraft (the payload) sitting at the top under the nose cone. At about sixty miles (100 km), the rocket's first stage burns out and drops to earth. The second stage fires, pushing the vehicle to orbital speed. From here on, everything that's left is, in fact, a satellite – an object orbiting the earth.

Keeping in mind that we are now in orbit, let's follow the remaining steps. The second stage burns out. Explosive bolts fire to detach it. Side panels hinge back. Springs push the two stages apart. The third stage ignites, pushing what's left into the final orbit. Once there, a turntable starts the payload spinning. Restraining clamps pop off. And another set of springs releases the spacecraft, which by now is the only functioning machinery at the end of a trail of discarded parts. Last of all, instrument covers (similar to the lens cap of a camera) are ejected to allow the spacecraft's sensors to start their job.

All in all, getting a satellite up and operating is a bit like opening a birthday package. You have to remove the card, ribbon, wrapping, box, and packing to get to the gift. A typical launch will leave two rocket stages, loose clamps, springs, bolts, panels, and covers – in addition to the payload – all floating around the earth.

Actually, there's even more junk than that. When explosive bolts fire to separate the stages, hundreds of metal fragments shoot out. If leftover fuel in one of the empty stages happens to explode, as it sometimes does, then the orbital lanes are strewn with thousands of chunks of metal. And as rocket parts bake in the fierce sunlight in space, the paint begins to flake off. One such high-velocity paint chip (the size of a grain of salt) struck the U.S. space shuttle in 1983 and gouged a pea-sized crater in one of the windows. There are probably billions of similar paint particles in earth orbit.

Film of astronauts floating in space may give the impression that everything up there is drifting harmlessly. But objects in low orbit are in fact jetting around at no less than 17,500 miles per hour (28,000 km/h), which is seven times faster than the speediest rifle bullet. Imagine what it would be like if all the junked cars, flat tires, hubcaps, soda cans, and other roadside trash not only stayed out on the highway after being discarded but kept moving at high speed with the traffic, and you will get a picture of the danger posed by orbiting debris. A head-on collision, even with a screw or a paint chip, could be disastrous.

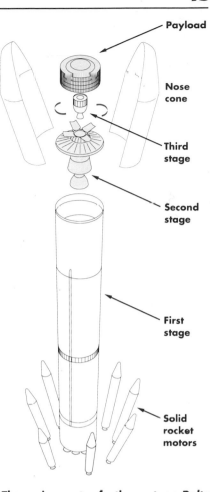

Payload

Nose cone

Third stage

Second stage

First stage

Solid rocket motors

The major parts of a three-stage *Delta* rocket. Everything from the second stage on (except the nose cone) usually ends up in orbit.

Bright fragments of metal, insulation, and ice surround this spacecraft (an *Apollo* lunar module) just after a separation maneuver.

Bigger than a deluxe mobile home, the *Skylab* space station was the largest piece of orbiting junk ever to fall to earth. It was unoccupied at the time.

Orbital Lifetimes

There is a natural force that cleans up much of the space trash: air. Even in the tiny quantities that exist in the lower reaches of space, air eventually slows satellites to below orbital speed and sends them plunging back through the atmosphere, where friction from the air heats them to metal-melting temperatures. Only the very heftiest chunks make it to the ground. One such chunk was the eighty-two-ton (75,000-kg) *Skylab* space station that broke apart on the way down and crashed in several pieces on Australia in 1979.

Most rockets enter orbit at a height of about 100 miles (160 km) where the air is a billion times thinner than air at sea level. Satellites at this altitude stay aloft for only a day or two before the faint but constant rush of air slows them enough to bring them falling back to earth.

Temporary as these low orbits are, they are well-suited for spy satellites, which must stay close to the earth in order to get detailed pictures. Every so often these low-flyers fire their thrusters to keep up to speed and stay in space.

A speck of white paint zipping through space chipped a window of the U.S. space shuttle in 1983. The impact made a crater ⅕ inch (5 mm) wide, damaging the outermost of the shuttle's three-layer window. The pane cost $50,000 to replace.

Normally, space vehicles use the 100-mile (160-km) zone to drop off bulky rocket stages on their way to higher orbits where the air is even thinner and a spacecraft's future is more secure. For example, at 200 miles (about 300 km) a satellite will stay aloft for several months; at 400 miles (650 km), for several decades; at 600 miles (1,000 km), for several centuries; and out at 10,000 miles (16,000 km), the estimated lifetime is a million years or more. In these very highest altitudes, air ceases to be a problem and the only resistance space vehicles encounter is from weak forces such as the moon's gravity and the pressure of sunlight.

The lifetimes given above are for circular orbits. For elliptical orbits, the situation is more complex. The oldest satellite currently in space is *Vanguard 1*, which was launched by the United States into a highly elliptical orbit on March 17, 1958, five months after the Soviets opened the space age by orbiting *Sputnik 1*. In a low orbit, *Sputnik 1* reentered after three months. But *Vanguard 1* was launched to last. On each orbit it soared up to an apogee of 2,466 miles (3,968 km). Then, during the second half of its orbit, it swung down to a perigee of 404 miles (650 km). In the more than thirty years that *Vanguard 1* has been looping up and down in this way, its apogee has dropped by less than fifty miles (80 km). Oddly, its perigee has stayed virtually the same. This may seem the opposite of what should happen, since most of the air that would cause the craft to slow down is on the perigee side of the orbit and one might expect that side to drop first.

Spacewreck: Sputnik 1

Launch: Oct. 4, 1957
Nationality: USSR
Last transmission: Oct. 25, 1957
Location: Low earth orbit, until reentry on Jan. 4, 1958

Like the first raft to test the oceans, the first ship to try out an earth orbit was a simple craft: an aluminum sphere, a transmitter, and a battery good for three weeks. Historic as it was, *Sputnik 1* was greeted by Americans with dismay as well as admiration. Few thought the Soviets were capable of leaping into space before the United States. But those familiar with the Soviets' pioneering rocket research, and their national obsession with space travel, were not surprised.

Sputnik 1 with scientist.

The external fuel tank of the U.S. space shuttle burns up during reentry over Hawaii in 1984. The faint streak at the upper right is the track of the orbiting shuttle. The distant glow on the horizon is an erupting volcano.

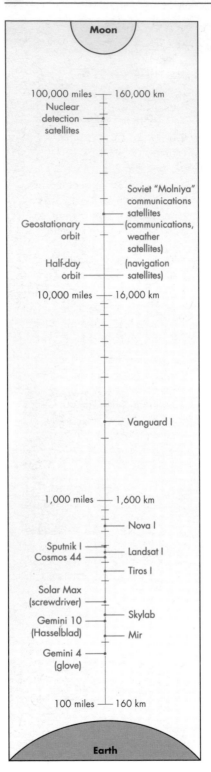

Altitude chart. Selected satellites discussed in the text are shown at apogee. Distances are not to scale; each major division of altitude is ten times larger than the one before.

But what actually happens is that as *Vanguard 1* races around the perigee at the bottom of its orbital ellipse, its speed decreases ever so slightly from air friction. With less energy to shoot up the wall of the gravity sink, *Vanguard 1*'s apogee is not quite so high during the next orbit, dropping by an average of two feet (60 cm). But even at the slightly lower apogee, the vehicle has exactly enough energy to fall to the same perigee as before.

Vanguard 1's apogee will continue to drop in this way for about 300 years until it has shrunk down to about the perigee height and the orbit is roughly circular. Then the air drag will be more evenly distributed around the orbit, and the orbit will begin to shrink evenly, like a deflating balloon. When the orbit has reached about 100 miles (160 km) above the earth, the end will be only a few days away. *Vanguard 1* will reenter the atmosphere in a blaze of glory sometime in the twenty-fourth century, a relic as ancient to the people of that day as the *Mayflower* is to us.

Space Wrecks

The chart at the beginning of this chapter shows that the densest region of satellites extends out to about 600 miles (1,000 km). Within this swarm are the usual odds and ends of rocket parts, as well as weather satellites, earth resources satellites, military satellites, scientific satellites, and usually one or more human-occupied satellites, such as the Soviet space station *Mir* or the U.S. space shuttle.

Like *Vanguard 1*, which sent its last transmission in 1964, most of these spacecraft no longer work. Even though they are regularly replaced by newer models, the old models still stay in orbit. A good example is *Cosmos 44*, which was launched by the Soviet Union in 1964 as an experimental weather satellite. (*Cosmos* is the catch-all name given by the Soviets to a broad range of spacecraft.) Functioning only a short while, *Cosmos 44* was soon replaced by *Cosmos 58* and *100* in 1965. These, in turn, were replaced by two more satellites in 1966, three in 1967, two in 1968, and two or three more (in the new *Meteor* series) in every year since. Almost all are still in orbit, mostly between 350 and 550 miles (600-900 km). Only two or three out of the more than sixty launched still actually work.

In the same region, you will also find *Tiros 1*, the first U.S. weather satellite, launched in 1960. *Tiros 1* stopped transmitting after eighty-nine days and was soon replaced by *Tiros 2, 3, 4, 5, 6, 7, 8*, and so on through many different models (eventually ending up with the name *NOAA* after the National Oceanic and Atmospheric Administration). There are now more than thirty. Only two work.

Further clogging the space shallows are over a hundred, mostly dead, navigation satellites orbiting at about 600 miles (1,000 km). Some of these guided ships and submarines at sea as far back as the 1960s. (Incidentally, the most recent American satellites in the series are called *Nova*.)

The strangest class of orbiting debris accumulates at roughly 250 miles (400 km), where human-piloted missions generally fly. If you could get at it, this would be the most useful junk in space. While out on a spacewalk during the *Gemini 10* flight in 1966, astronaut Mike Collins misplaced an expensive, Swedish-made Hasselblad camera with dozens of exposed pictures. It became, if nothing else, Sweden's first satellite. A year earlier, astronaut Ed White lost a glove (easy to lose on the ground, too) during his spacewalk. In 1984, a power screwdriver escaped from the American space shuttle during a satellite-repair mission. Unfortunately, these handy items have all reentered and burned up.

U.S. shuttle astronaut James Van Hoften wields a Japanese power screwdriver while repairing the *Solar Max* satellite in 1984. The screwdriver later escaped into space.

The first American spacewalk may have lasted just 20 minutes, but astronaut Ed White managed to lose a glove before he was safely back inside.

If it could be melted down, all of the junk in space would make an object about as heavy as a U.S. Navy frigate like this one.

Then there is the actual garbage in space – plastic bags full of it that are regularly tossed out of the Soviet space station *Mir*. Fortunately, this stuff quickly loses altitude and is incinerated in the atmosphere.

Is outer space filling up with discards and trash? One way of looking at it is that the total mass (weight) of all human-made objects now in earth orbit and beyond comes to about 3,000 tons (2½ million kg). It may seem like a lot, but this is the weight of a frigate, a small warship that carries 200 sailors. If you dismantled a frigate and scattered the pieces all over the world, you would be hard put to find any trace of the ship. Think how more completely lost the pieces would be in the far vaster regions of space.

So if the combined mass of all objects now in space is the equivalent of one small ship, it should be no surprise that the space shuttle goes up for a week and finds nothing else there – except perhaps an occasional paint chip. It's true that anything that came along would pose a risk of catastrophe. But practically nothing has, at least not yet.

Spacewreck: Landsat 1

Launch: July 23, 1972
Nationality: USA
Last transmission: Jan. 16, 1978
Location: Earth orbit at 560 miles (900 km)

Landsat 1 was the first spacecraft to focus on what could be learned about earth resources from orbit. In the picture of southern California at right (taken on March 14, 1973), you can pick out cultivated fields, forests, mountains, snow-cover, desert, and cities, not to mention the ominous San Andreas fault – a stark line running across the middle of the frame above Los Angeles (at lower right). Vegetation is shown as red. So successful was *Landsat 1* that four other *Landsats* and several similar craft from other nations have followed.

Landsat 1 **snaps a picture of Los Angeles and environs, one of millions of scenes photographed during the craft's 5½-year life.**

Remember that a marble-sized object traveling at orbital speed packs the punch of a hand grenade. Radar on earth can detect objects as small as a baseball in low orbit. But smaller objects – and there are certainly plenty of them – pass unnoticed. With the space lanes gradually filling up, they could strike at any time. In 1981, a Soviet navigation satellite was mysteriously blown into hundreds of bits, possibly by just such a collision.

Climbing Higher

Above 600 miles (1,000 km), the population of satellites decreases sharply. We think of satellites as operating outside of the earth, but most are in fact focussed on our planet and so stay fairly close in order to do their job. They are either watching, listening to, or otherwise participating in activities going on down below – activities that can range from prospecting for minerals, to eavesdropping on military communications, to manufacturing new medicines under the unique conditions of weightlessness.

As we climb higher, space vehicles take longer to complete their orbits. The reason is partly that they have a greater distance to go in their much larger circles. But as we travel farther and farther from earth, the gravitational pull of the earth decreases. At twice the distance (measured from earth's center), gravity is one-quarter as strong. At three times the distance, gravity exerts one-ninth the pull.

A *Vanguard* spacecraft sits atop its launch vehicle, one of the smallest ever used to launch a satellite. This *Vanguard* didn't make it into space, but three others (beachball-sized or smaller) were successfully orbited in 1958 and 1959. All three are still up.

The Soviet space station *Mir* in orbit. A ferry ship for the crew is attached at the right. The entire complex is 84 feet (26 m) long. Trash is ejected through an airlock in the side of the station.

It All Adds Up

How big is a trillion? To visualize it, let's start with a number one billion times smaller: a thousand. There are about a thousand (1,000) type characters, including word spaces, in this box. A fast typist can make these 1,000 keystrokes in two minutes flat.

Twenty Thousand Leagues Under the Sea, a 300-page novel, represents almost a million (1,000,000) keystrokes. Working non-stop, our typist can polish off the Jules Verne classic in thirty-three hours.

Four complete sets of the *Encyclopedia Britannica,* at thirty-two volumes a set and 1,000 pages a volume, make up a collection of a billion (1,000,000,000) letters and spaces. A superhuman typist could accomplish this job in about four years, working non-stop.

Finally, the million or more volumes in the library of a typical large university represent roughly a trillion (1,000,000,000,000) letters and spaces. Hitting keys at a rate of 1,000 every two minutes, day and night, our intrepid typist would be clicking away, volume after volume, for close to 4,000 years.

With less gravity tugging at a spacecraft, less speed is needed to stay in orbit, and a satellite takes longer to go around. Another way of looking at it is that the slope of the gravity sink flattens out as we go higher.

In a 100-mile (160-km) circular orbit, for example, a satellite takes 88 minutes to complete an orbit. At 200 miles (320 km), gravity has weakened a bit, the circumference of the orbit is slightly larger, and a satellite takes 91 minutes to go around once. Out at 600 miles (970 km), an orbit takes 104 minutes.

Gravity keeps falling off and the orbital period (the time for one revolution) keeps lengthening as we climb. At 12,500 miles (20,000 km), one orbit takes twelve hours – half a day. In this region can be found swarms of the latest American and Soviet navigation satellites – amazing machines that can pinpoint locations on the ground to within thirty feet (10 m).

A satellite in a half-day orbit retraces roughly the same pattern over the earth's surface – called the "groundtrack" – every day. It may rise in the west at noon, cross overhead, and set in the east at 6:00 pm. The next day it rises at about the same time and place. Such regularly-repeating orbits are called *synchronous* orbits. They are geared to an exact fraction of the earth's period of rotation and are possible at different altitudes. For example, a satellite in a circular orbit at 160 miles (260 km) has an orbital period which is exactly one-sixteenth of a day, or 1½ hours. At the end of the spacecraft's first orbit, the earth has turned 22½ degrees to the east, and the spacecraft is flying over an area to the west of its original path. Each orbit shifts westward by 22½ degrees until, on the seventeenth orbit, the earth has turned 360 degrees (one complete rotation) and the entire pattern starts over again. The advantage to anyone tracking the satellite from the ground is that it flies overhead on a dependable schedule.

The higher the synchronous orbit, the slower the satellite will be moving and the longer it will stay in view of someone on the ground. In the half-day orbit, a satellite takes several hours to cross the sky, while in the one-sixteenth-day orbit, it takes only a few minutes.

In practice, synchronous orbits become unsynchronized over time due to the combined effects of air friction, earth's slight bulge at the equator (which causes orbits to "wobble" a bit), and the fact that earth rotates slightly more than 360 degrees in a twenty-four-hour day (as it curves part way around the sun in its orbit). These effects make it difficult to achieve a perfectly synchronous orbit, though they pose less of a problem the higher you go.

The Geostationary Belt

There is not much above the half-day circular orbit, until we get to 22,300 miles (35,900 km). Up to now in our journey, satellites have been scattered about the earth like bees around a hive. Some payloads circle the equator. Others loop north and south between the polar regions. The vast majority orbit at some angle in between. But when we reach 22,300 miles (35,900 km) the swarm of satellites forms a thin band surrounding the planet like a slim version of Saturn's ring. This is known as the *geostationary belt* – the one-day synchronous orbit – where a satellite travels at the same rate as the turning earth and so appears to be stationary in the sky.

This effect, however, works only over the equator because only there will an orbit run exactly due east (the same direction that the earth turns). A spacecraft cannot follow one of the other east-west lines around the earth (the latitude lines) because then the vehicle would have to orbit around an off-center point inside the planet. This means that it's impossible to make a satellite geostationary over, for example, Moscow. To do so, the satellite would have to follow the 55½-degree latitude line where Moscow is located, which would require it to orbit a point in the top half of the earth. This is as impossible as playing a record with an off-center hole. Satellites must orbit an object's center.

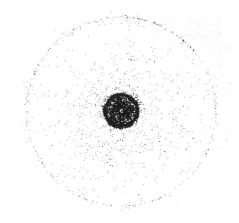

Satellites swarm around the earth in this computer-generated view from over the north pole for October 14, 1988. The near-perfect ring, about one-tenth of the distance to the moon, is the geostationary belt.

METEOSAT   1983 MONTH 3 DAY 15 TIME 1155 GMT (NORTH) CH. VIS 2
NOMINAL SCAN/RAW DATA   SLOT 24   COPYRIGHT - ESA -

The earth viewed from geostationary orbit, 22,300 miles (35,900 km) above the equator. About one-third of the planet is visible at this altitude: in this case, Africa, Arabia, Europe, and part of South America. The photograph was made by *Meteosat 2*, a weather satellite for the European Space Agency.

Six geostationary satellites, photographed from the ground. In the five minutes during which this exposure was made, the earth turned 1¼ degrees. The satellites moved exactly the same angle and so show up as points on the photo. The stars didn't move and so show up as streaks. The two satellites at the far right seem to be close neighbors but are in fact 870 miles (1,400 km) apart.

The earlier example of a spacecraft rising in the west at noon and setting in the east at 6:00 pm is how a satellite in a half-day synchronous orbit over the equator, headed east, would appear. If that spacecraft were boosted up to 22,300 miles (35,900 km) – the altitude for a one-day orbit – it would never rise or set at all. Instead it would appear to hover in a single spot of sky as it moved eastward in perfect step with the rotating planet below. Antennas need only to be aimed at that spot and never moved again.

Interestingly, to put a satellite into this zone takes as much fuel as traveling to Mars or Venus. But since 1964, vehicles have been lining up to get there because of the commercial advantages of a "fixed" communications post in space.

First was *Syncom 3*, launched in time for the 1964 summer Olympic Games. Hovering over the international dateline in mid-Pacific, *Syncom 3* took in a view that extended from Mongolia to Montana. Television signals could be sent from the Olympics in Tokyo up to the satellite and then relayed live to the United States. So novel was this technique that it was used only for the opening ceremonies. "Live via satellite" had a very special meaning in those days.

Now, of course, television transmission from the geostationary belt is commonplace – along with radio, telephone, weather photos, stock reports, newspaper transmission, and other services. Next time you notice a moment's delay in a long-distance telephone call, think about how your voice is being routed through space. Since the radio signal that carries your

Earth-Locator Chart

Next time you're lost in the stars, you can find your way home by looking for nine planets orbiting a medium-bright star in the outskirts of a spiral galaxy called the Milky Way. Head for planet three (the blue one).

conversation travels at only 186,000 miles per second (300,000 km/sec) – the speed of light – it takes a half second or so for your words to reach the other phone through a geostationary satellite, and for the reply to get back to you.

Or think of it the next time you watch television, especially cable television which is relayed largely through satellites. That old movie on the Disney Channel – the 1950s classic starring James Mason as Captain Nemo – is coming to you from *Galaxy 1*, hovering 22,300 miles (35,900 km) above the Pacific Ocean – the very waters where the *Nautilus* began its last, fateful voyage.

Climbing past the more than 300 payloads and other objects currently in the geostationary belt, we soon reach the apogee of the satellites used by the Soviets to relay most of their television signals. These craft loop from a low point of 400 miles (600 km) over the southern hemisphere up to a dizzying 25,000 miles (40,000 km) over the arctic – a twelve-hour round trip during which the orbiters can broadcast for about eight hours to the Soviet Union. Such highly elliptical orbits give the Soviets better coverage for the extreme northern part of their country than they can get from geostationary satellites over the equator, far to the south.

Past that, there is very little: a scientific satellite here and there; at 75,000 miles (120,000 km), a few military payloads designed to detect the brilliant light of nuclear explosions down on earth; and then nothing, until we reach the moon.

Electronic signals travel in straight lines; the most direct way to transmit from one side of the curved earth to another is through a point that can be seen by both, such as a geostationary satellite. These satellites have the advantage of being visible over a very wide area and they are fixed relative to the ground.

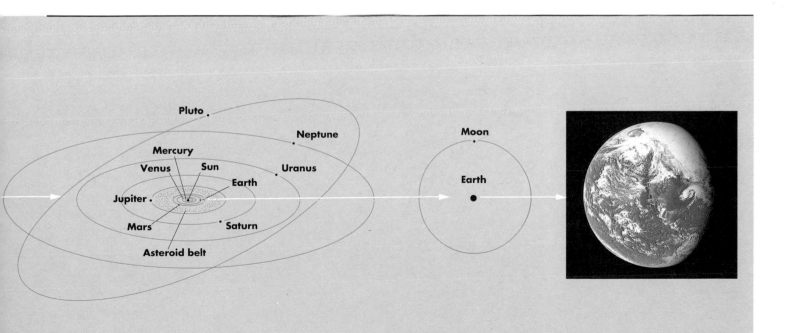

An Offshore Island

On July 16, 1969, three astronauts set off on a trip to that most substantial satellite of the earth, the moon.

Their giant rocket – a *Saturn 5* – boosted them into a "parking" orbit near the earth, where they checked all systems and then re-lit their third stage. The added thrust increased their speed by about half to 24,250 miles per hour (39,030 km/h), fast enough to take them on a highly elliptical path out to the moon, 240,000 miles (380,000 km) away.

It was fast indeed, for the astronauts noted that they could see the earth rapidly growing smaller, "a sobering, almost melancholy sight," one of them later recalled.

Blasting out of a circular orbit at 119 miles (191 km), within seven minutes they had climbed to the 250-mile (400-km) altitude where Mike Collins dropped a Hasselblad camera three years earlier. Collins himself was aboard *Apollo 11* for this trip, along with Neil Armstrong and Buzz Aldrin.

Three minutes later, *Apollo 11* shot through the most congested region of satellites at 600 miles (1,000 km). In another twelve minutes, it coasted past the lonely apogee of *Vanguard 1*, one of the first satellites ever launched, at 2,400 miles (3,900 km).

Climbing the hill of earth's gravity sink, *Apollo 11* was fast losing speed. It would take two more hours to reach the geostationary altitude of 22,300 miles (35,900 km), where satellites orbit at the same rate as the turning earth. Twenty years ago when Armstrong, Aldrin, and Collins passed this ring that stretches 165,000 miles (266,000 km) around the planet, it held only a dozen payloads. Now it has hundreds.

Not that the astronauts could see anything anyway. The chances of spotting a satellite on the way to the moon are about equal to seeing a whooping crane in your backyard – it could happen, but don't count on it.

◄
The *Saturn 5* rocket used to launch the *Apollo* moon expeditions. Note the size of the workers on the launch tower.

The third stage of the *Saturn 5* with open adapter panels. One such panel may have given rise to a mysterious sighting during *Apollo 11*'s journey to the moon.

Wreck Chart: Moon

The map shows locations of space-craft currently on or orbiting the moon (exact orbits are not shown). They are listed below by year of launch. Flyby probes and rocket stages are omitted. Note that numbers 2, 13, 17, 19, and 41 crashed on the moon's "far side", the side that is always turned away from the earth. Spacecraft numbers 16, 36, 38, and 45 were last heard from in low lunar orbits and have probably crashed. Spacecraft number 21 is known to have crashed but the exact site is not known.

1959
✳ 1. Luna 2, USSR*

1962
✳ 2. Ranger 4, USA (crashed on far side)

1964
✳ 3. Ranger 6, USA
✳ 4. Ranger 7, USA*

1965
✳ 5. Ranger 8, USA*
✳ 6. Ranger 9, USA*
✳ 7. Luna 5, USSR
✳ 8. Luna 7, USSR
✳ 9. Luna 8, USSR

1966
▲ 10. Luna 9, USSR*
● 11. Luna 10, USSR*
▲ 12. Surveyor 1, USA*
✳ 13. Lunar Orbiter 1, USA * (deliberately crashed on far side)
● 14. Luna 11, USSR
✳ 15. Surveyor 2, USA
✳ 16. Luna 12, USSR* (orbiter, probably crashed)
✳ 17. Lunar Orbiter 2, USA* (deliberately crashed on far side)
▲ 18. Luna 13, USSR*

1967
✳ 19. Luna Orbiter 3, USA* (deliberately crashed on far side)
▲ 20. Surveyor 3, USA*
✳ 21. Lunar Orbiter 4, USA* (deliberately crashed somewhere on near side)
▲ 22. Surveyor 4, USA
● 23. Explorer 35, USA*
✳ 24. Lunar Orbiter 5, USA* (deliberately crashed)
▲ 25. Surveyor 5, USA*
▲ 26. Surveyor 6, USA*

1968
▲ 27. Surveyor 7, USA*
● 28. Luna 14, USSR*

1969
✳ 29. Luna 15, USSR
■ 30. Apollo 11, USA * (descent stage and equipment)
■ 31. Apollo 12, USA * (descent stage and equipment)

1970
▲ 32. Luna 16, USSR* (descent stage of automatic sample-return)
▲ 33. Luna 17, USSR* ("lunokhod" automatic rover)

1971
■ 34. Apollo 14, USA* (descent stage and equipment)
■ 35. Apollo 15 , USA* (descent stage and equipment)
✳ 36. Apollo 15 Subsatellite, USA* (released in orbit by Apollo 15, probably crashed)
✳ 37. Luna 18, USSR

✳ 38. Luna 19, USSR* (orbiter, probably crashed)

1972
▲ 39. Luna 20, USSR* (descent stage of automatic sample-return)
■ 40. Apollo 16, USA* (descent stage and equipment)
✳ 41. Apollo 16 Subsatellite, USA* (released in orbit by Apollo 16, crashed on far side)
■ 42. Apollo 17, USA* (descent stage and equipment)

1973
▲ 43. Luna 21, USSR* ("lunokhod" automatic rover)
● 44. Explorer 49, USA*

1974
✳ 45. Luna 22, USSR* (orbiter,probably crashed)
▲ 46. Luna 23, USSR

1976
▲ 47. Luna 24, USSR* (descent stage of automatic sample-return)

North

✳ 2, 13, 17, 19, 41

▲ 33
✳ 1
■ 35
▲ 43
■ 42
✳ 29
▲ 46 ▲ 47
▲ 18
✳ 9 ✳ 8
▲ 10
✳ 3
✳ 15 ▲ 26 ▲ 25 ✳ 5 ✳ 37
✳ 24 ▲ 39
✳ 7 ▲ 20 ▲ 22 ■ 30 ▲ 32
▲ 12 ■ 31 ■ 34
■ 40
● 11, 14, 23, 28, 44
✳ 4 ✳ 6

▲ 27

South

Key
✳ Crashed
▲ Soft landing
■ Human landing
● Orbiting
* Mission success (the spacecraft accomplished all or most of its objectives)

No Passing

The lack of landmarks gave the journey an eerie quality, according to one astronaut. "The strangest aspect of the trip out," said Alan Bean, who flew to the moon aboard *Apollo 12* in November 1969, "is that you don't really pass anything on the way. You leave the launch pad, then you leave earth orbit, and about a couple of days later, after passing nothing, all of a sudden you're where you were going. That lack of way points had the effect of making it seem a little magical or mystical getting there."

Even so, the *Apollo 11* crew did see something. At around 212,000 miles (341,000 km), during the third day out, they spotted "an L-shaped object" through their low-power telescope, like "an open book" or "an open suitcase." At times it looked like a hollow cylinder. No one ever figured out what it was. Most likely it was a panel from their discarded third stage. But there was nothing else in sight with which to compare it, so the astronauts couldn't tell how large it was, or how far away, or how fast it was moving. Eventually it disappeared.

Coincidentally or not, *Apollo 11* was about to pass through the point where the moon's gravitational pull becomes stronger than that of the earth – where the ship would begin a slow fall into the shallow lunar gravity sink. It is possible for objects to accumulate near the top of this sink, pulled equally by the earth and moon and so, for a time, going toward neither.

Apollo 11 was now traveling 2,039 miles per hour (3,281 km/h), down from the 24,250 miles per hour (39,030 km/h) that it was traveling when it left parking orbit. Its speed would now gradually increase as it coasted "downhill" to the moon, 39,000 miles (63,000 km) away.

Target Moon

We might take a moment to consider the target of this trip. Like the metal-hulled *Apollo* spaceship itself, the moon was once a part of the earth, or so many scientists believe. According to this theory, the moon was excavated 4½ billion years ago when an object the size of Mars plowed into the primitive earth and hurled a massive jet of debris far into space. Eventually this rubble collected into single body to form the moon – 2,200 miles (3,500 km) in diameter and 6,800 miles (11,000 km) in circumference.

Meanwhile, large fragments of the shattered earth regrouped to form the planet we now know – 8,000 miles (13,000 km) in diameter and 25,000 miles (40,000 km) in circumference, or four times the moon's dimensions.

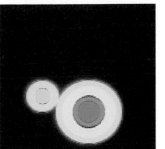

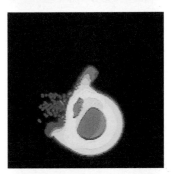

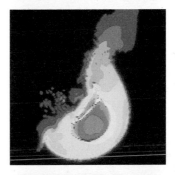

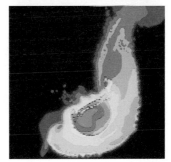

A Mars-sized chunk of rock collides with the earth (top), launching a large jet of debris into space. This computer simulation covers the first thirty minutes of a cataclysm that may have produced the moon. The fragmented shapes eventually formed back into spheres under the influence of gravity.

Other theories argue that the moon spun off in a less dramatic way. Or that it formed somewhere else, passed close to the earth, and was then captured in orbit. Or that it was pieced together at the same time and place as the earth from the same cloud of rocky material. But for now, many scientists favor the collision theory. That event launched a large chunk of our planet into space with a billion billion times the energy of the *Saturn 5* rocket, making the moon the biggest piece of junk out there.

At almost one-quarter million miles (400,000 km), it is also one of the most distant objects orbiting our planet. A few satellites are in ellipses that take them a bit farther, but there is not much farther to go without gliding right out of earth's gravity sink and into solar orbit. Following the rule that the greater the distance from the object being orbited, the longer the orbit takes, the moon takes 27½ days to circle the earth, or roughly one month.

The moon's enormous size and stately speed would seem to make it an easy target from earth. But the first few probes that tried to hit the moon missed. The problem can be understood if we consider our sink model. At the lunar distance, the earth's gravity sink flattens to a gentle slope. Within this slope, moving along at 2,200 miles per hour (3,500 km/h), is a rather large but not very deep depression with the moon at the bottom. A satellite

Pow! Earth litter collides with the moon. The empty third stage of a *Saturn 5* rocket was intentionally crashed into the moon to provide data for seismometers on the surface. The crater made by this bus-sized vehicle shows up as a tiny hole, 130 feet (40 m) wide, surrounded by a spray of black debris.

must careen up earth's gravity sink to the flatter outskirts and then hit the lunar depression at exactly the right spot and speed. Once in, the spacecraft either falls directly to the bottom and hits the moon, or curves along one side and misses. If a miss (which is what *Apollo 11* intended), then the craft can fire a braking rocket to slow itself and be captured into lunar orbit, or it can do nothing and automatically shoot back out of the lunar sink.

The first to succeed at this game of moving-pocket billiards was the Soviet probe *Luna 2*, which crashed into the Man in the Moon's right eye on September 14, 1959, after a flight of thirty-four hours. Future visitors will know the historic spot by its fresh-looking crater, fifty feet (15 m) wide.

Many crash-landers, soft-landers, and orbiters followed during the next decade. A look at the lunar wreck chart on page 28 shows how thoroughly the moon was explored during this era. In order to pave the way for human explorers, the moon was mapped, measured, probed, and analyzed. The names of the spacecraft tell the story: *Ranger*, *Surveyor*, *Lunar Orbiter* – all American; equally daring were the Soviet craft, most named *Luna*. Among other things, these machines proved that the moon was neither inhabited, nor highly-explosive, nor a bottomless dust bowl, as some had predicted. Many left their marks as swimming pool-sized craters in the lunar crust.

Landing the Eagle

When *Apollo 11* rounded the moon and fired its braking rocket on July 19, 1969, it joined seven other objects – five *Lunas* and two American craft – then orbiting the moon. These included a mysterious Soviet probe that had arrived two days earlier on an unknown mission.

Since the moon has no atmosphere, objects can orbit at practically any height. One of the Soviet ships was regularly dipping to within sixty miles (100 km) of the surface, and losing no altitude to air resistance, as would quickly happen over the earth. *Apollo 11* transferred to this low region and then detached a landing vehicle (called the lunar module, or LM). The LM transferred to an even lower orbit, taking it to within ten miles (16 km) of the surface, again without a trace of air resistance.

Just as *Apollo 11* had reached the moon through a series of transfer orbits, going from a low circular orbit around the earth to a high elliptical orbit, it was now descending to the moon through a similar series of orbit changes.

Spacewreck: Surveyor 3

Launch: Apr. 17, 1967
Nationality: USA
Last transmission: May 4, 1967
Location: On the moon

The fourth craft to land successfully on the moon, *Surveyor 3* was the first to take a jab at the lunar soil, showing it to be as soft as a freshly-plowed field in Iowa. The fact that the automatic landers didn't sink out of sight was assurance that astronauts (due to arrive in 1969) wouldn't either. Below is the best portrait of a remote-landing probe on the moon. Who took the picture? Alan Bean of *Apollo 12*, whose fellow crew member, Pete Conrad, is standing just out of view to the right, casting the long, slender shadow.

Surveyor 3 in the spot where it skidded to a rough landing on the moon in 1967.

The final step was to leave orbit altogether. So the LM turned on its braking rocket and began the final descent to the surface, keeping its motor running all the way down to cushion the fall.

Apollo 11's LM, called *Eagle*, had a surprisingly hair-raising descent. Because of small irregularities in the moon's mass (which create gravitational "bumps" in the lunar sink), *Eagle* overshot its intended landing site and headed for a dangerous boulder field. Armstrong, at the controls with co-pilot Aldrin, searched for a safer spot, while running low on fuel.

With less than thirty seconds of gas left – and then an uncontrolled fall – *Eagle* finally set down. It was July 20, 1969, at the western edge of the Sea of Tranquility, part of the Man in the Moon's left eye. The first humans to touch the moon had arrived just a few weeks short of the tenth anniversary of *Luna 2*'s historic crash, almost crashing themselves. Meanwhile Mike Collins orbited overhead in the mother ship.

The following day the Soviet mystery orbiter also descended to the lunar surface, but a bit more violently. It plowed into the ground 700 miles (1,100 km) northeast of *Eagle*. Not yet ready for a human landing, the Soviets had sent a sophisticated automatic probe, but only succeeded in adding another crater to the lunar scenery.

The *Apollo 12* lunar module, 60 miles (100 km) above the moon, prior to landing. Note the moon's sharply-outlined edge that shows no trace of an atmosphere.

Roving for Rocks

Armstrong and Aldrin set about exploring the moon in a highly-compressed version of the explorations that are done on earth. In a little over two hours, they put up instruments, collected rocks, shot photos, took a call from their boss (the President), performed experiments, and all the while described what they were seeing and how they were coping in the new environment.

One of their chief aims was to collect as many rocks as possible. To make room for the samples, they left behind as much equipment as they could. Consequently, when the "bug-head" section of the LM, called the ascent stage, took off for the mother ship the next day, considerable junk, in addition to the hulking, two-ton (1,800-kg) descent stage, was left sitting on the lunar surface. Today you will still find:

1 television camera on tripod
1 stereo camera
1 Hasselblad camera
miscellaneous geology tools
assorted covers, fasteners, packing materials, and canisters
2 life-support backpacks
2 pairs lunar overshoes
armrests and other unneeded items from the LM
commemorative medals from earth
1 American flag

Also left are a seismometer that relayed data on "moon quakes" to earth for three weeks and a laser reflector that is still used as a target for laser pulses shot from earth to measure the earth-moon distance.

In five later *Apollo* landings between 1969 and 1972, junk would accumulate to a total of twenty tons (18,000 kg) – about what a small used-car lot represents. Since the later missions stayed longer, set up more experiments, ranged farther afield, and brought back more rocks, they also left behind a richer assortment of merchandise, including two golf balls, an astronaut pin, a falcon feather, a tiny statue representing astronauts killed in the line of duty, a family photo, and the "moon buggies"– electric-powered, two-seater cars used for getting around. These vehicles covered about twenty miles (30 km) each during the last three landings, allowing astronauts to investigate some very rough terrain. If you can thread your way through the lunar mountains to the lovely valleys where the missions set down, just bring a fresh thirty-six-volt battery: the cars are parked in neutral and ready to roll.

Objects left on the moon: an astronaut car, a family photo, and research instruments.

Mister Rogers holds a replica of the toothbrush that drifted into space on a return trip from the moon in 1971. Astronaut Al Worden (right) was aboard the *Apollo* mission that deposited this unusual item of space junk.

The Soviets achieved some of the same feats as the Americans without sending humans to do the driving and collecting. In a triumph of robotics, they landed two remote-controlled rovers that toured a total of thirty miles (48 km) of the lunar landscape. The Soviets also obtained their own lunar samples from three sites where their rockets set down, scooped up material, and then returned to earth. (The Soviet mystery mission during *Apollo 11*'s visit was probably a failed sample-gathering attempt.)

Returning to earth from the moon is a matter of repeating the flight in reverse. For *Apollo 11*, the ascent stage of the LM launched into a low elliptical orbit, then transferred to the same circular orbit as the mother ship, and then reconnected with it. Crew and cargo all collected inside the mother ship, which then blasted out of the lunar sink and into the big basin that leads down to earth.

Left behind by *Apollo 11* was a historic item: the ascent stage of *Eagle*, which probably crashed about a year later – not from air resistance but from the faint tug of the distant earth (which gradually pulled the craft's orbit out-of-round causing it to crash). Later missions would deposit a couple of scientific satellites in orbit around the moon before they departed. These, too, have no doubt crashed.

Spacewreck: Lunokhod 1

Launch: Nov. 10, 1970
Nationality: USSR
Last transmission: mid-Sept. 1971
Location: On the moon

One of the few robot probes that actually looks the part, *Lunokhod 1* lumbered down the ramp of its descent stage like a tank invading Omaha Beach. For the next eleven lunar days (lasting 29½ earth days each), *Lunokhod 1* roamed in, out, and around craters, conducting experiments and taking thousands of photos. This is surely how machines will explore more distant worlds such as Mars. At dawn on the twelfth day, *Lunokhod 1* failed to respond to radio commands from earth, having apparently succumbed to the extreme cold of the long lunar night.

Lunokhod 1, officially known as Luna 17.

And for a time – a little over two days in August 1971 – an ordinary toothbrush and comb were coursing through space in the wake of one returning *Apollo* mission, objects which floated through an open hatch during a spacewalk and then down the earth's gravity sink to a fiery and glorious farewell, back home in the atmosphere.

The ascent stage of *Eagle* in lunar orbit. Left behind when the astronauts returned to earth, this object has almost certainly crashed by now. Most of the later *Apollo* missions intentionally crashed their ascent stages.

The Deep

The orbits of the innermost planets shrunk down to the scale of the Pacific Ocean. Distances in space are 11,000 times greater than those shown on the map. For example, the distance from earth to the moon is represented as Los Angeles to Santa Catalina Island – or 22 miles (35 km). The actual distance is 240,000 miles (380,000 km).

Twenty-two miles (35 km) off the coast of southern California is Santa Catalina, a high, rocky island two hours by ferry from Los Angeles. If we suppose that this twenty-two-mile (35-km) span represents the distance between earth and the moon, then the orbit of Venus – the closest planet to earth – is more than a week's voyage by steamship to Hawaii. The orbit of Mercury is some 2,800 miles (4,500 km) farther at remote Ocean Island. And the sun, according to this model, sits in the blistering Australian outback one-third of the way around the globe from Los Angeles.

So you can think of space in the direction of the sun as being as vast, empty, and difficult to cross as the Pacific Ocean. The moon is just off-shore by these standards. Space in the other direction – toward the outer planets – is unbelievably more vast. But we will get to that later.

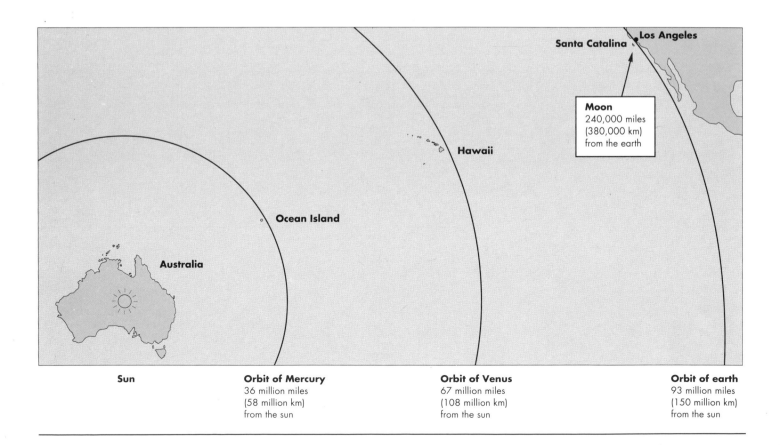

Los Angeles

Santa Catalina

Moon
240,000 miles
(380,000 km)
from the earth

Hawaii

Ocean Island

Australia

Sun	Orbit of Mercury	Orbit of Venus	Orbit of earth
	36 million miles (58 million km) from the sun	67 million miles (108 million km) from the sun	93 million miles (150 million km) from the sun

Testing the Deep

Vehicles began to test the deep water beyond the moon not long after the launch of the world's first satellite in 1957. On January 4, 1959, *Luna 1* sailed past the moon at sufficient speed to escape the earth's gravity field and enter solar orbit. Launched by the Soviet Union, *Luna 1* was apparently intended to hit the moon as its successor *Luna 2* triumphantly did nine months later.

But no matter. If earth satellites are "artificial moons" (as they used to be called) then *Luna 1* had become an artificial planet orbiting the sun. It was the first human artifact to leave our world and go its own way in the solar system. Its own way takes it halfway up to the orbit of Mars and then back down to the orbit of earth every 446 days, which is *Luna 1*'s "year," or period of revolution around the sun. As of mid 1989, *Luna 1* had completed twenty-five of these years. It can expect billions more as long as it doesn't hit either the earth or moon, which may occasionally get in the way.

Unfortunately, *Luna 1* stopped transmitting after 2½ days, providing only a few clues about the state of interplanetary space. Several later probes were more durably in touch. *Pioneer 5*, launched by the United States in 1960, transmitted from an orbit between earth and Venus for 107 days. *Venera 1*, launched in the direction of Venus by the Soviets the following year, got to 14 million miles (23 million km) from earth before going dead. Both gave valuable information about the ebb and flow of atomic particles from the sun known as the "solar wind." These bits of atoms race through space at up to two million miles per hour (3 million km/h) and pose a hazard to any humans who happen to be beyond earth's magnetic field. Earth's magnetic field traps particles of the solar wind in two donut-shaped regions extending out to 11,000 miles (17,000 km); particles that make it through this barrier crash into the atmosphere at the north and south magnetic poles, producing the northern and southern lights.

The most spectacular interplanetary probe up to its time was the American ship *Mariner 2*, which was launched toward Venus in August 1962. In December of that year, the hardy 440-pound (200-kg) craft flew past Venus at a distance of 22,000 miles (35,000 km) and made the first close-up measurements of another planet. The news was not particularly inviting: earth's nearest neighbor turned out to have surface temperatures of at least 800 degrees Fahrenheit (425°C), far surpassing the hottest kitchen oven.

The earth and moon, photographed by a probe in deep space. *Voyager 1* took this picture from a distance of 7¼ million miles (12 million km) while on its way to Jupiter in 1977.

Wreck Chart: Venus

The map shows locations of spacecraft currently on or orbiting Venus (exact orbits are not shown). They are listed below by year of launch. Flyby probes, rocket stages, and vehicles that disintegrated in Venus's thick atmosphere are omitted. The location of spacecraft number 1, the first to hit another planet, is not known. The map is based on radar measurements made through Venus's permanent cloud cover.

1965
* 1. Venera 3, USSR (location unknown)

1967
* 2. Venera 4, USSR*

1969
* 3. Venera 5, USSR*
* 4. Venera 6, USSR*

1970
▲ 5. Venera 7, USSR*

1972
▲ 6. Venera 8, USSR*

1975
● 7. Venera 9 Orbiter, USSR*
▲ 8. Venera 9 Lander, USSR*
● 9. Venera 10 Orbiter, USSR*
▲ 10. Venera 10 Lander, USSR*

1978
● 11. Pioneer Venus 1, USA (radar mapper, still operating)*
* 12. Pioneer Venus 2 Large Probe, USA*
* 13. Pioneer Venus 2 North Probe, USA*
* 14. Pioneer Venus 2 Day Probe, USA*
* 15. Pioneer Venus 2 Night Probe, USA*
▲ 16. Venera 11 Lander, USSR*
▲ 17. Venera 12 Lander, USSR*

1981
▲ 18. Venera 13, USSR*
▲ 19. Venera 14, USSR*

1982
● 20. Venera 15, USSR (radar mapper)*
● 21. Venera 16, USSR (radar mapper)*

1984
▲ 22. Vega 1, USSR (Venus-lander portion of Comet Halley probe)*
▲ 23. Vega 2, USSR (Venus-lander portion of Comet Halley probe)*

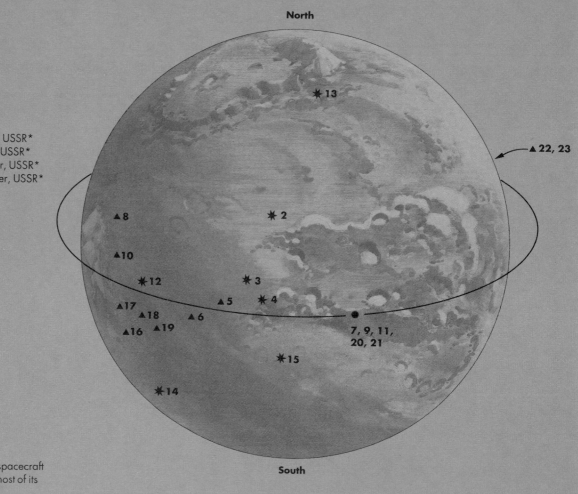

Key
* Crashed
▲ Soft landing
● Orbiting
* Mission success (the spacecraft accomplished all or most of its objectives)

The Hohmann Route

Mariner 2 blazed the interplanetary trail in more ways than one. It was the first to demonstrate the practicality of a route based on the *Hohmann transfer ellipse*. This is a fuel-saving trajectory to the planets first proposed by the German engineer Walter Hohmann in 1925. It is none other than the elliptical transfer orbit we discussed in the second chapter.

There, if you recall, we learned that the path that connects one circular orbit to another is an ellipse. An ellipse that fits exactly between two circular orbits – touching one at the six o'clock position and the other at twelve o'clock – makes a perfect Hohmann trajectory that will use the least energy in getting from one planet to another.

Because the orbits of the planets do not lie on exactly the same plane (as they appear to do when drawn on a flat sheet of paper), nor are they perfect circles (being ever-so-slightly elliptical), the ideal Hohmann route must usually be modified. This was the case with *Mariner 2*.

But modified or not, Hohmann trajectories are the simplest and most economical paths to the planets. They are the sea lanes of deep space. And just as there are favorable and unfavorable seasons for setting out on the old sailing routes, there are good and bad times for making use of the Hohmann routes. The planets have to be in exactly the right positions.

For instance, when embarking on a Hohmann transfer trip to Venus, the earth must be fifty-four degrees ahead of Venus at the time of launch so that the spacecraft and planet arrive at the intersection of their orbits at the same time. Viewed from overhead, the situation looks like this: at launch, earth is at six o'clock and Venus at eight o'clock (the numerals are in the usual places on this "clock," but the planets and spacecraft travel counterclockwise, the prevailing direction of travel in the solar system); Venus, moving more quickly on its inside orbit, pulls even with earth at three o'clock; the spacecraft is slightly ahead here; planet and probe gradually draw nearer, their paths converging; at twelve o'clock they meet.

The probe can fire a rocket at this point to break its speed and get captured in orbit around Venus. Or it can expend even more energy and land. Or it can do nothing and continue past Venus in solar orbit. Meanwhile, earth lags behind at the one o'clock position.

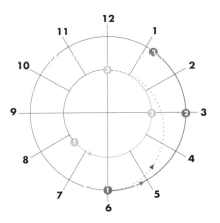

The Hohmann "clock":
(1) Earth launches a mission to Venus when Venus lags behind.
(2) Venus catches up with earth.
(3) The spacecraft and Venus meet, while earth lags behind.

Spacewreck: Helios 2

Launch: Jan. 15, 1976
Nationality: W. Germany
Last transmission: Mar. 3, 1980
Location: Solar orbit

Every 187 days, *Helios 2* reaches a point 27 million miles (43 million km) from the sun, putting it closer to the bottom of the solar sink than any other spacecraft, or indeed any planet. At such a distance the sun is twelve times brighter than the sun as seen from earth. Covered with mirrors that reflect most of the sizzling radiation, parts of the craft still get as hot as 680 degrees Fahrenheit (360° C), hot enough to melt lead. *Helios 2* orbited through this infernal region eight times, relaying data about the blast of solar particles, before finally going dead.

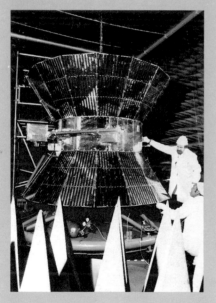

German engineers prepare *Helios 2* for a mission to the sun.

If we tried launching when the earth and Venus were closest to each other, at three o'clock, Venus would be well ahead when the probe crossed its orbit at nine o'clock. Most people think that you should simply cross in a straight line when the planets are closest. But the resulting orbit makes such a steep angle with the solar gravity sink that no existing upper-stage rocket could supply the necessary speed. Even if you could transfer onto such a slope, your ship would be going so fast that you would have little time to look or slow down as you zipped past the target.

The earth-to-Venus Hohmann trajectory works for any pair of planets. For targets that are higher up the gravity sink from the launch planet, imagine the situation in reverse: Venus launches a mission to earth at twelve o'clock when earth is at one o'clock; spacecraft and earth meet at six. (Only, flip the clock over backwards so that everything continues to run counterclockwise.)

Remember, by the way, that there is no difference between traveling up or down the gravity sink. Both take rocket energy. Anything launched from earth shares earth's orbital motion around the sun and so, for Hohmann orbits, must expend energy in order to slow down and fall into a lower solar orbit – just as it must expend energy to speed up and get into a higher orbit.

There are two scheduling limits connected with the Hohmann route. One is the *launch interval*. The other is *time-of-flight* to the target planet. The launch interval is the number of days between favorable line-ups, when launches can be made – the "launch opportunity". For example, it takes 584 days for earth and Venus to come around to their six o'clock and eight o'clock positions. The time-of-flight is how long it takes to travel the route – for example, 146 days from earth to Venus.

The table below gives these times for space voyages to the planets.

Least-Energy (Hohmann) Trajectories from Earth

Planet	Launch interval	Time-of-flight	
Mercury	116 days	105	days
Venus	584 days	146	days
Mars	780 days	259	days
Jupiter	399 days	2¾	years
Saturn	378 days	6	years
Uranus	370 days	16	years
Neptune	367 days	31	years
Pluto	367 days	31-46	years

There is some leeway in these numbers. A launch opportunity, or *launch window*, opens at the intervals shown in the center column. But the window is open for several days or weeks depending on how much extra fuel is available to make up for a late start. As for time-of-flight (shown in the last column) faster trips are possible, again depending on how much extra fuel is put aboard the ship. A faster trip requires a larger ellipse which intersects the orbit of the target planet sooner. In the past, the Soviets have preferred faster trips with smaller payloads because of the shorter lifespan of their equipment. With generally more reliable machines, Americans have been able to put their probes on slower, more fuel-efficient routes.

Notice a very interesting thing: according to the table, the launch opportunities to faraway Pluto occur twice as frequently (once a year) as those to much-closer Mars (once every two years). If you've ever jogged on a running track, you probably know the reason. It takes longer to "gain a lap" on someone who is running about your speed than with someone who is walking. After passing your closely-matched competitor, you may have to run two or three more laps before catching up again. But you pass the person who is walking practically every time you go around. It's much the same in space. The nearby planets are more closely matched with earth and it takes a while for one planet to pass another – or be passed. But the more distant planets are going more slowly, and earth catches up about once a year.

Space Champ: Pioneer 6

Launch: Dec. 16, 1965
Nationality: USA
Last transmission: Still operating
Location: Solar orbit

Long after other payloads of its generation have died, *Pioneer 6* keeps sending back data from its path between the orbits of Venus and earth – almost a quarter of a century after launch. The secret of its success? Partly the shape. Like all cylindrical satellites, *Pioneer 6* spins to stay stable. And once set spinning, the craft keeps rotating indefinitely. No propellants are needed to keep the antenna in position to transmit to earth. The only problem is finding the time on over-booked earth antennas to tune in to this satellite that just won't quit.

Pioneer 6 with instrument booms folded for launch. The craft is about the size of a trash barrel.

Spacewreck: Viking 2 Lander

Launch: Sept. 9, 1975
Nationality: USA
Last transmission: Apr. 12, 1980
Location: On Mars

Viking 2 Lander sits in a boulder field 100 miles (160 km) west of the Martian crater Mie, at a latitude comparable to Seattle, Washington on earth. The photo below was made three weeks after landing, in late September 1976. At that time *Viking 2 Lander* and its sister ship *Viking 1 Lander* (on the opposite side of the planet) were in the midst of experiments to detect life on Mars. No life turned up.

Viking 2 Lander looks over its shoulder at the red planet (more accurately, the brown planet). The weather on this typical sunny summer afternoon was about -20 degrees Fahrenheit (-30° C) with light winds.

Gravity Assist

Following several successful Hohmann and modified-Hohmann runs to the planets in the 1960s and early 1970s (flybys of Venus in 1962 and 1967, flybys of Mars in 1964 and 1969, and a Mars orbiter in 1971), American space officials were ready to try a more ambitious trajectory called the "gravity assist."

It's easy enough to use the gravity sink of a planet to change the direction of a spacecraft. Simply by dipping into the sink and coasting out again, the probe's path is bent. But because the gravity sink is moving (sweeping along with the planet around the sun), a spacecraft also gets a push that can either speed it up or slow it down depending on which side of the planet it passes. The gravity assist is a way of changing the craft's direction and speed without using any fuel at all. It's the same as firing a rocket to change course.

By studying the different possibilities offered by this technique, engineers discovered that in 1974 Venus and Mercury would be in position for a double planetary mission. A space probe could fly a normal route to Venus and then get redirected to the innermost planet, Mercury, for free. This mission was accomplished according to plan by the spacecraft *Mariner 10*.

Wreck Chart: Mars

The map shows locations of space-craft currently on or orbiting Mars (exact orbits are not shown). They are listed below by year of launch. Flyby probes and rocket stages are omitted.

1971
- 1. Mars 2 Orbiter, USSR*
- ✳ 2. Mars 2 Lander, USSR
- 3. Mars 3 Orbiter, USSR*
- ▲ 4. Mars 3 Lander, USSR*
- 5. Mariner 9, USA*

1973
- 6. Mars 5, USSR*
- ▲ 7. Mars 6 Lander, USSR

1975
- 8. Viking 1 Orbiter, USA*
- ▲ 9. Viking 1 Lander, USA*
- 10. Viking 2 Orbiter, USA*
- ▲ 11. Viking 2 Lander, USA*

1988
- 12. Phobos 2, USSR
(designed to release two lander probes on Martian moon, Phobos; contact lost in Mars orbit, 1989)

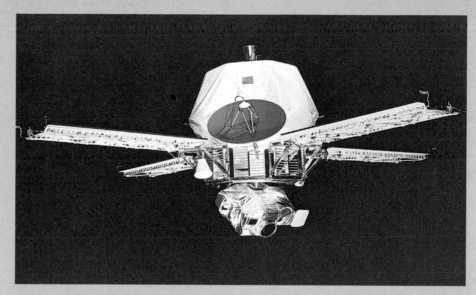

Mariner 9, orbiting Mars since 1971.

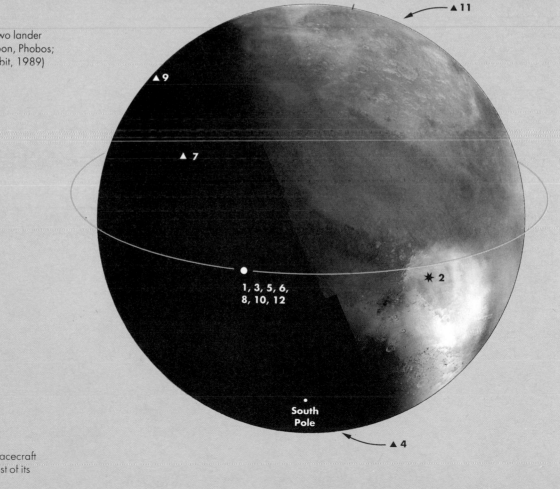

Key
- ✳ Crashed
- ▲ Soft landing
- ● Orbiting
- * Mission success (the spacecraft accomplished all or most of its objectives)

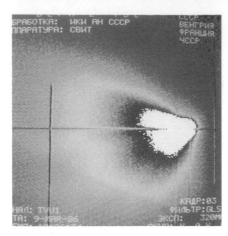

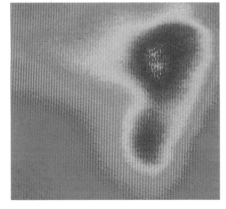

Halley's Comet, a natural piece of solar-system debris, photographed by the Soviet probe *Vega 2* in March 1986. (Below) A close-up view of Halley's icy, peanut-shaped nucleus, which is about ten miles (16 km) long. Colors in both photos are added to help interpret the data.

The gravity assist is a way around a serious problem that shows up in the last column of the Hohmann schedule on page 41. Note that the Hohmann travel time to Jupiter is 2¾ years, which is not unbearably long. But getting to the planets beyond Jupiter takes longer than most people are willing to wait: 6 years to Saturn, 16 to Uranus, and 31 to Neptune. However, a gravity assist at Jupiter, which has the deepest and most powerful gravity sink of any of the planets, can greatly speed up a journey, as we will soon see.

Junk Among the Planets

Meanwhile, back in the inner solar system, things are beginning to get crowded. A rough count of where different probes have traveled as of mid 1989 (whether they worked or not) shows the following.

Spacecraft to the Inner Planets

	Flyby	Orbiter	Lander (hard and soft)
Mercury	1	–	–
Venus	8	5	18
Mars	10	7	5

Of the flyby probes, all are still somewhere in solar orbit. No one knows exactly where. Of the orbiters, all are probably still circling. All of the landers are sitting on the surface in some state, either crunched (the hard landers) or intact (the soft).

Not listed are thirty-five loose rocket stages, mostly drifting in orbits between Venus and Mars, plus about a dozen scientific probes in the same vast region. Five of these made measurements of Halley's Comet when it passed through in 1986; two flew past Venus first, dropping off surface and atmospheric probes, and using the gravitational assist of Venus to reach Halley. Not yet at its destination is *Magellan*, launched from earth in May 1989 and due to go into orbit around Venus in August 1990.

Also somewhere out there are six moon-bound spacecraft that missed, a Mars-bound ship entombed in its rocket nose cone (which never detached), and the lunar module ascent stage of *Apollo 10*, a dress rehearsal for *Apollo 11* that did everything but land.

Fewer than ten of these one-hundred-plus objects are working spacecraft.

The Far Flyers

Completing the census are four spacecraft that are truly in a class (and place) by themselves. All four have been to Jupiter – 390 million miles (630 million km) from earth. Three have traveled past Saturn, twice as far as the distance to Jupiter. One of these has been to Uranus – 1.7 billion miles (2.7 billion km) from home – as well as past Neptune, in the outer limits of the solar system at 2.7 billion miles (4.4 billion km) from earth.

If we use the "Pacific Ocean" model at the beginning of this chapter, such distances are far off the map. Using twenty-two miles (35 km) to represent the distance to the moon, Jupiter is the equivalent of one and one-half times around the earth's 25,000-mile (40,000-km) circumference; Saturn is three times around; Uranus, six times around; and Neptune, ten times. And these are only the most direct courses that do not take into account the elliptical paths that spacecraft must travel to reach their destinations.

In the Hohmann schedule on page 41, we saw that trips to the outskirts of the solar system should take several decades. But these four ships managed it in less than half the usual time, with considerably less rocket fuel than it would normally take.

They did it with the help of Jupiter, the great slingshot of the solar system. A dip in and out of Jupiter's massive gravity sink, second only to the sun's, can more than double a spacecraft's speed, giving a hefty push up the solar sink. One of the probes used the push at Jupiter to reach Saturn, the push at Saturn to continue on to Uranus, and the push at Uranus to go on to Neptune.

All four of these explorers – two named *Pioneer* and two named *Voyager* – are climbing out of the solar sink, never to return. And they are hardly junk: all four continue to point their antennas at a tiny blue point that is earth, relaying information about conditions at the far-distant frontiers of our planetary system.

Eventually the four ships will fly out of the region dominated by the solar wind and into the faint breeze of particles from other suns, which we call stars. With luck, they will still be operating when they get there – five, ten, or possibly more years from now. In many thousands of centuries, going their various ways, they will travel beyond some of the nearest stars.

Pioneer 10, **now the most distant object launched by humans, gets some last-minute attention before departing for space in 1972.**

At the end of *Twenty Thousand Leagues Under the Sea*, the *Nautilus* is trapped in a deadly whirlpool off the coast of Norway. Spinning ever faster in tighter and tighter circles – like a satellite spiraling back to earth – Captain Nemo and his crew disappear into the vortex. Although Jules Verne leaves their fate unclear, it would seem that his unforgetable characters join the ranks of the wrecked on the ocean floor.

Our intrepid ships, too, are caught in a vortex, only one that is vastly larger. For billions of years, long after the sun has died and the earth has vanished, the two *Pioneers* and the two *Voyagers* will plow the waves of interstellar space, orbiting the center of the great whirlpool of stars called the Milky Way.

The Nautilus and its lifeboat are trapped in a whirlpool at the end of *Twenty Thousand Leagues Under the Sea*. The book's narrator and two others escape in the boat.

M83 – a galaxy very much like our own. Our solar system makes one complete revolution around the galactic center every 200 million years. *Pioneer 10* and *11*, and *Voyager 1* and *2* will do the same.

Where Are They?

There is no better way to understand how far *Pioneer 10* and *11*, and *Voyager 1* and *2* have ventured than to make a scale model. You will need only paper, a drawing compass, and a ruler at least thirty-six inches (or one meter) long.

With the compass, draw a circle with a radius (or half diameter) of one inch (25 mm). This will represent the orbit of Mars. Earth, the moon, Venus, Mercury, and the thousands of satellites, probes, and rocket parts that we've studied are all within this small circle.

If you like, draw in the orbit of earth at ⅔ inch (17 mm) from the center; Venus, at ½ inch (12 mm); and Mercury, at ¼ inch (6 mm). At this scale, the moon is two-thousandths of an inch (0.04 mm) from the earth. The center of the circle represents the sun.

Now take a yardstick and mark it at 20 inches (52 cm), 21 inches (53 cm), 28 inches (70 cm), and 32 inches (82 cm). Place the stick flat on the paper measuring from the sun. The 20-inch (52-cm) mark will show the distance of the probe *Pioneer 11* in June 1990. Launched from earth in April 1973, *Pioneer 11* took a modified-Hohmann route to Jupiter, arriving in late 1974. Flung backwards and accelerated across the solar system by Jupiter's gravity, *Pioneer 11* passed Saturn in 1979, the first probe to do so.

On our model, Jupiter is 3½ inches (9 cm) from the sun; and Saturn, 6 inches (16 cm).

Now mark the line that connects *Pioneer 11* with the sun. Consider this as twelve o'clock. Move the ruler to the eleven o'clock position and measure out to 21 inches (53 cm). Here is the June 1990 location of the probe *Voyager 2*. Taking advantage of a planetary alignment that occurs only every two centuries, *Voyager 2* left

earth in 1977, visited Jupiter in 1979, Saturn in 1981, Uranus in 1986, and Neptune in August 1989.

On our model, Uranus is 13 inches (32 cm) from the sun; and Neptune, 20 inches (50 cm).

Sister ship *Voyager 1* can be found at one o'clock. Raise the yardstick up from the sun at an angle of about 30 degrees (the angle between two adjacent numerals on a clock is 30 degrees). June 1990 will find *Voyager 1* – launched within a few weeks of *Voyager 2* in 1977 – at a distance of 28 inches (70 cm), on a northerly route after passing Jupiter in 1979 and Saturn in 1980.

Finally, 32 inches (82 cm), measuring along the six o'clock position, marks the

spot where the most remote object launched by humans will exceed the farthest distance achieved by the farthest planet. On about June 18, 1990, *Pioneer 10*, which departed earth some eighteen years earlier, will climb beyond the highest point on the sun's gravity sink reached by Pluto, the most distant known planet. The first to venture past the orbit of Mars, through the asteroid belt, past Jupiter, and the first to escape from the solar system, *Pioneer 10* is truly a pioneer.

One more measurement: imagine counting out to 175,000 inches (about 3 miles, or 4½ km). That's the distance on our scale model to the nearest star – a distance *Pioneer 10* will cover in 112,000 years.

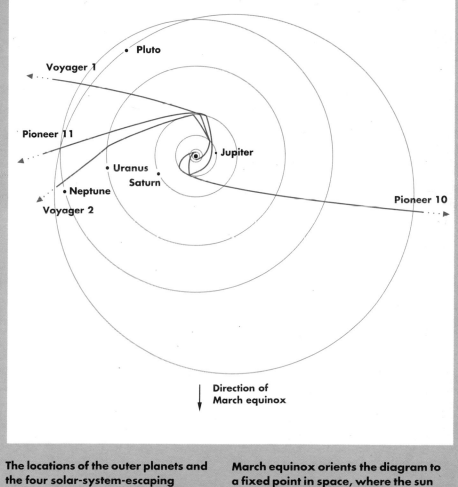

The locations of the outer planets and the four solar-system-escaping spacecraft in June 1990. The innermost circles are the orbits of Mars, earth, Venus, and Mercury. The **March equinox orients the diagram to a fixed point in space, where the sun appears in the sky from earth on the first day of spring.**

Further Reading

Books

Arthur C. Clarke, *The Promise of Space* (Berkley, New York, 1985). The mechanics of space flight clearly presented by the famous science fiction author and father of satellite communications.

Kenneth Gatland, *The Illustrated Encyclopedia of Space Technology* (Crown, New York, 1981). Separate chapters on various kinds of spacecraft – weather, interplanetary, manned lunar, etc. – all excellently illustrated.

Desmond King-Hele, *Observing Earth Satellites* (Van Nostrand, New York, 1983; currently out-of-print but available from *Sky & Telescope* magazine, below). Binoculars, a stopwatch, and a lawn chair are all you will need to track satellites from your backyard. A veteran observer for over thirty years explains how.

Magazines

Sky & Telescope (Sky Publishing, Cambridge, MA). Faithful, in-depth reporting of all space missions related to astronomy, and some others as well. Includes occasional reviews of computer programs for satellite tracking.

Spaceflight (British Interplanetary Society, London). Covers space programs of all nations. Most issues feature a detailed listing of recent satellite launches.

Aviation Week & Space Technology (McGraw-Hill, New York). Space news for space professionals. Coverage of military missions often spills secrets. Known as *Aviation "Leak"* for this reason.

Index

Credits

Except as noted below, photographs are courtesy of NASA, and drawings are by Matthew Bartholomew. We are grateful to one and all.

Front cover drawings Terry LeBlanc; **5, 46** (top) Jules Verne, *Twenty Thousand Leagues Under the Seas,* George M. Smith & Co., Boston, 1873; **10, 18** Jeanne Lee; **9** photo by R. Sluder and G. Boquist for Technology International; **11** (bottom) A. de Saint Exupéry, full credit on page 2 of this book; **14** (right) **23** (top) Teledyne Brown Engineering; **17** (right) **21** (bottom), **34** (bottom), **44** (top) Tass/Sovfoto; **17** (bottom), **24** (left) © Paul D. Maley; **20** (top) Bath Iron Works; **23** (bottom) European Space Agency; **24** (bottom, both) Palomar Observatory, California Institute of Technology; **28** (photo) Lick Observatory; **29** M. Kipp and J. Meloch; **34** (top) Family Communications, Inc.; **43** (planet photo) U.S. Geological Survey; **44** (bottom) Space Research Institute, Moscow; **46** (bottom), David Malin, © Anglo-Australian Telescope Board, 1986.